The Golden Age of the AMERICAN POSTER

"...the great periods of art were those in which it allied itself most intimately with the daily life of the people, and in this craze for posters, 'the poor man's picture gallery,' as they are called, is seen almost the first sign of a renaissance in which the spirit of the century, which is so largely a commercial one, will find an utterance in beauty instead of ugliness."

Claude Fayette Bragdon,
quoted in *Poster Lore*, 1896

"The kiss of Fame and art for art's sake were his goal
  When Chromer, painter, with the world first went to cope;
But now he barely pays for bread and board and coal
  By making lurid posters for Van Apple's soap."

Anonymous

The Golden Age of the AMERICAN POSTER

A CONCISE EDITION OF *THE AMERICAN POSTER RENAISSANCE*

VICTOR MARGOLIN

BALLANTINE BOOKS · NEW YORK

For my parents
and for Sylvia

Copyright © 1975, 1976 by Victor Margolin

All rights reserved. No part of this publication
may be reproduced or used in any form or by any means—graphic,
electronic, or mechanical, including photocopying, recording, taping,
or information storage and retrieval systems—without
written permission of Watson-Guptill Publications, a
division of Billboard Publications, Inc., New York,
N.Y. 10036. Published in the United States by Ballantine
Books, a division of Random House, Inc., New York, and
simultaneously in Canada by Ballantine Books of Canada,
Ltd., Toronto, Canada. Originally published as
American Poster Renaissance, 1975.

Library of Congress Catalog Card Number: 75-4813

ISBN 0-345-25129-6-695

This edition published by arrangement with Watson-Guptill
Publications, a division of Billboard Publications, Inc.

Manufactured in the United States of America

First Ballantine Books Edition: October 1976

Contents

Acknowledgments

An historian must be something of a detective, with a taste for following up clues and tracking down odd bits of information. During the course of writing this book, I was fortunate to encounter a group of people who kindly shared their knowledge with me, directed me to poster sources, and, in several cases, loaned me material from their own collections.

Robert Brown loaned me his copy of *Das Frühe Plakat*, an invaluable German catalog of 1890s posters. I am indebted to essays on the 19th century poster by Dr. Edgar Breitenbach in the book *The American Poster*, and by Roberta Wong in her catalog for the exhibition "American Posters of the Nineties." Susan Thompson of the Columbia University School of Library Science told me about the Engel Collection of the Columbia University Libraries, probably the most complete collection of late 19th century American posters in the United States. Robert Nikirk, Librarian of the Grolier Club, shared the resources of the Grolier Club library with me. Roberta Wong of the Print Division at the New York Public Library, who is an authority on Will Bradley, gave me much help in checking facts and details about posters and artists.

Kenneth Lohf, Head of Special Collections of the Columbia University Libraries, made the Columbia poster collection available to me. During the long hours of selecting and photographing the posters, I was helped immensely by members of his staff: Bernard Crystal, Mimi Bowling, and Henry Rowan.

At the Library of Congress, I thank Alan Fern, Chief of the Prints and Photographs Division and his staff members: Milt Kaplan, Elena Millie (Curator of the Poster Collection), Jerry Kearns, and Leroy Bellamy. Other museums and archives which furnished advice or photographs include the Chicago Historical Society, the Metropolitan Museum of Art, the New York Public Library, the Currier Gallery of Art in Manchester, New Hamphire, and the Hopkins Center Art Galleries at Dartmouth College.

Ray Wapner and Justin Schiller of Justin G. Schiller Ltd., dealers in posters and children's books, loaned me a hard-to-find Victoria Bicycle poster by Will Bradley, and Leslie and Alice Schreyer made available several items from their collection. Donald Manza photographed all the posters at Columbia University and from the private collections.

Lastly, I thank the editorial staff at Watson-Guptill for their help and suggestions; Don Holden, Editorial Director, Diane Casella Hines, Associate Editorial Director; and my editor, Sarah Bodine.

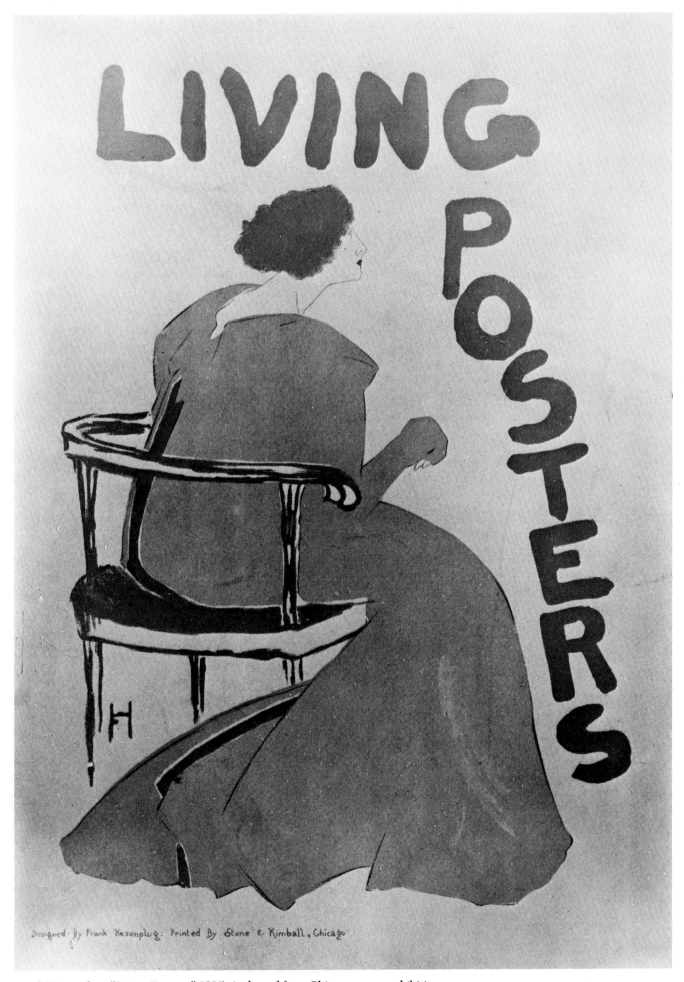

Frank Hazenplug, "Living Posters," 1897. A placard for a Chicago poster exhibition.

THE CHRISTMAS SCRIBNER'S

Poem by Rud~
yard Kipling

Six illustrated
stories by Joel
Chandler Harris
Henry van Dyke
and others

Poem by James
Whitcomb Riley

The Workers by
Walter A. Wyckoff

The Art Features
include Christmas
frontispiece by A.
B. Frost · 8 pages
in colors by A. B.
Wenzell · 21 Re~
productions of Sir
E. J. Poynter's work

Special Christmas
Cover in 9 colors
by Maxfield Parrish

Maxfield Parrish, *Scribner's*, c. 1900.

Introduction

During the 1890s, the poster in America came into its own as a medium of artistic expression. Although it had long been the handmaiden of commerce, the poster was considered merely a means of advertising until the late 1880s and was not thought to have any intrinsic artistic value.

But the popularity of the new artistic posters by Chéret, Grasset, Toulouse-Lautrec, and others in Paris convinced several American publishers that an appealing placard, prominently displayed in booksellers' windows, on walls, and on hoardings, might increase the sales of their magazines. When the artistic posters proved as popular in America as in Europe, other publishers commissioned them to promote their books, newspapers, and periodicals.

The American poster renaissance flourished for a few brief years in the 1890s. The leading patrons were the publishers, but manufacturers, impressed by the commercial success of the new posters, soon climbed on the bandwagon. Before the decade ended, posters by leading American artists and designers had been used to tout bicycles, patent medicine, and even dynamite.

It is doubtful that the poster movement would have thrived without the bursting energy and momentous changes that characterized the 1890s. Business was expanding in all directions and great cities rose to become the centers of financial power. Thousands of migrants from rural areas as well as millions of aspiring immigrants from Europe flocked to the cities to find more stimulating and remunerative employment. Intellectuals and artists also came to the cities seeking outlets for their work among the magazines, newspapers, book publishers, and theaters that were springing up to inform and divert the urban population. Though many poster designers of the 1890s had fine arts backgrounds, most were making their living as commercial artists in the large urban centers.

The decade had opened on a note of prosperity, but financial speculators, flooding the country with false securities, precipitated the Panic of 1893. Banks, corporations, and mortgage companies failed and unemployment spread. By 1897 the Panic had waned, but not before new organizations were formed to protect the interests of the workers: the Populist Party, the Socialist Labor Party, and the American Federation of Labor.

Undaunted by the nation's economic difficulties, the World's Columbian Exposition opened in Chicago in May 1893. Young Maxfield Parrish journeyed all the way from Philadelphia to see the fair. He wrote to his mother: "These stupendous architectural groupings could scarcely be surpassed in fairy tales without becoming absurd." The Columbian Exposition symbolized a spirit of change and helped create a fitting climate for the almost simultaneous emergence of the artistic poster in America.

Edward Penfield's poster for a book of stories about the masses of New York City, 1896.

Jules Chéret's posters exuded the *joie de vivre* of Belle Epoque Paris.

European Origins

The roots of the artistic poster stretch back to early 19th century France. In Paris, a new type of popular book was responsible for the poster revival that occurred in the 1830s and 1840s. Booksellers, who were often also publishers, displayed small posters in their shop windows and on the boulevards to advertise the illustrated books they sold in installments. The posters were usually enlarged book illustrations, printed as monochrome lithographs, with text added. Their creators were the best-known book illustrators of the day: J. J. Grandville, Gavarni, Tony Johannot, Gustave Doré, Raffet, Nanteuil, and Edouard de Beaumont. Balzac attested to the interest of "those maniacs called collectors" when he wrote in *Illusions perdues* that the placards were "a poem for the eye and often enough an unpleasant surprise for the purse of their admirers." By 1850 the book poster had declined. Edouard Manet's illustrative black and white placard for Champfleury's *Les Chats* in 1869 is a rare example.

An early French book poster by Tony Johannot. This is one of eight hundred illustrations he created for Cervantes' novel.

Also in 1869, Jules Chéret printed the first color poster in France. Chéret, known as the "father of modern lithography," established the poster as an art form. Before him, posters were either lithographed illustrations or scenes resembling genre paintings transferred to stone by anonymous craftsmen. Chéret was the first to understand that the poster was meant for the street and not the gallery. To attract attention it had to be bold and simple.

Most lithographers of Chéret's day were skilled technicians who specialized in reproducing the paintings and drawings of others. But Chéret eliminated these middlemen and made his own drawings directly on the stone. By experimenting with new techniques, he created the subtle shadings and textures that characterized his style.

Chéret was a self-taught artist who began as a printer. In 1856, as a young man of 20, he went to England to study the more advanced technique of chromolithography. Ten years later he returned to Paris and opened his own firm. His first poster, a monochrome, publicized *La Biche au bois*, a play starring a 22-year-old actress named Sarah Bernhardt. From 1869 to 1888, Chéret worked in three colors, but after that he never used less than four or five. Though theaters, museums, and newspapers all commanded his talents, he is most closely identified with the music halls and cabarets that blossomed in Montmartre during the 1880s and 1890s. Chéret's frothy figures, who seem to defy gravity as they float joyously in space, are the quintessence of Belle Epoque exuberance. The artist was awarded a Légion d'Honneur in 1889 for creating a new branch of art by applying artistic techniques to commercial and industrial printing. By 1891, Chéret had created over 1,000 posters. As standards of poster production declined toward the end of the century, he abandoned lithography for pastel and oils.

Edouard Manet's placard for Champfleury's *Les Chats*.

Although Chéret was a technological innovator, he was also a classicist who found his inspiration in the painting of earlier periods, particularly the French rococo. Eugène Grasset, a contemporary of Chéret, looked even farther back to the tranquil art of the Middle Ages. Grasset was more interested in the decorative arts than in painting. He had been influenced by the English Arts and Crafts Movement, whose guiding spirit, William Morris, was also an ardent medievalist. Grasset displayed his fondness for the medieval period in designs for furniture, jewelry, textiles, books, and stained glass. His first poster was designed in 1886 and he subsequently received many commissions from both sides of the Atlantic. Although Grasset preferred to cling to tradition and vowed that there could never be a "new art," the curving lines, flat two-dimensional modeling, and subjective colors of his posters nevertheless made them the forerunners of Art Nouveau.

The term Art Nouveau is usually used to connote the decorative style that developed in France in the late 19th century and then spread to other countries. In graphic art, its predominant elements are a swirling line, an attention to ornamental detail, and an emphasis on the flat surface rather than modeling in depth. The artist who most reflected the Art Nouveau style in England was Aubrey Beardsley; in America it was Will Bradley.

Bonnard, Toulouse-Lautrec, and Steinlen, who were less intrigued by Art Nouveau, shared a common interest in the contemporary life of Paris, particularly the bustling activity of Montmartre. Toulouse-Lautrec's posters chronicled the gaiety of the cafés and music halls. Steinlen's usually depicted the two subjects dearest to him, his little daughter and his cats. And his many lithographs, which didn't have to please a patron, portrayed deep interest in the poor workers of his *quartier*. The notable artistic quality of the French poster in the 1890s was due to the revival of interest in color lithography by these artists and their predecessors among the Impressionists.

Ernest Maindron's *Les Affiches illustrées* (1886), an erudite history of the poster in France, stimulated public interest in collecting and confirmed the poster as a respectable art form. The journal *La Plume*, founded in 1889, published an occasional article on the poster and held regular exhibitions at its gallery, the Salon des Cent. Collectors found their mecca at the shop of Edmond Sagot, whose catalog, published in 1891, listed more than 2,200 different posters for sale. By the end of 1891, posters were being bought and sold in Brussels, London, and New York.

Félix Vallotton designed this woodcut placard for Edmond Sagot, the Paris poster dealer.

Posters in America

The popularity of the French posters did not go unnoticed by American publishers. In 1889, Harper & Bros. commissioned Eugène Grasset to do a cover for *Harper's Bazar* and two holiday posters for *Harper's Magazine*. The selection of Grasset, though commendable on artistic grounds, was a calculated concession to Puritan morality since his curly-locked cherubs, in contrast to the gay revelers of Jules Chéret, were certain not to offend a prim public. The same year, Louis Rhead, an English artist who had been in America since 1886, was asked to do holiday posters for the magazines *The Century* and *St. Nicholas*.

In November 1890, enthusiasts saw a large selection of French posters at the first poster exhibition in America, sponsored by the Grolier Club. They were impressed by the colorful placards of Chéret and Grasset which outshone the few realistic posters by American lithographers, particularly Matt Morgan.

Encouraged by the enthusiastic reception of their holiday posters, Harper & Bros. made the momentous decision in the early months of 1893 to publicize *Harper's Magazine* with a monthly placard. The assignment fell to Edward Penfield, a young illustrator and art director for the company. Critics usually date the beginning of the American poster movement from the appearance of Penfield's *Harper's* posters beginning in March 1893.

Other magazines soon began to commission posters on a regular basis, although *Harper's* was the only magazine with posters by a single designer until late 1894, when *Lippincott's* hired Will Carqueville. Penfield's posters, and those commissioned by other magazine and book pub-

Will Bradley's sketch for a billboard-sized theatrical poster. The gigantic lettering, which was designed so that it could be changed for later productions, was intended to capture the public's attention. Courtesy the Metropolitan Museum of Art. Gift of Mrs. Fern Bradley Dufner, 1952.

The young woman on Maxfield Parrish's 1896 *Century* poster *(top)* appeared two years later on a Spanish placard advertising sausages *(immediately above)*.

lishers, were small in size since they were designed for bookshop windows and newsstands rather than the hoardings.

The poster contest was a way of discovering new talent as well as drumming up publicity for the sponsor. The winning artists earned substantial prizes and a good deal of acclaim. The losers benefited little since their designs were usually kept by the sponsoring firm and sometimes used for promotional exhibitions. One irate artist, who received an announcement from a dried-fruit firm for a poster contest in which only one prize would be awarded and all the entries would become the property of the firm, sent the following reply: "Gentlemen—I am offering a prize of fifty cents for the best specimen of dried fruit and should be glad to have you take part in the competition. Twelve dozen boxes of each fruit should be sent for examination, and all fruit that is not adjudged worthy of the prize will remain the property of the undersigned."

Maxfield Parrish was a frequent winner of poster competitions. In 1896 the Pope Manufacturing Co. sponsored a contest for a poster to advertise the Columbia bicycle. Parrish's poster was considered the best of 525 entries and earned him the first prize of $250. That same year Parrish received second prize in *The Century*'s contest for a midsummer holiday poster. He might have had the first prize, which went to J. C. Leyendecker, but entries had been restricted to three colors and Parrish, an avid experimenter with the new halftone process, employed five.

A few American connoisseurs were already buying French posters as early as 1890, but the collecting mania didn't begin until 1893, when the mass-circulation magazines started to issue their monthly placards. Publishers soon realized the popularity of the posters and began printing extra copies for sale to collectors. Free posters were also offered to attract new subscribers.

Although many magazines were sold by subscription, there was still a brisk newsstand sale that was boosted significantly by the new posters sent to the dealers. When the newsdealers discovered that the artistic posters were of such interest to collectors, they began selling them instead of displaying them as the publishers had intended. Booksellers followed the same practice, eventually discouraging many publishers from issuing further posters. In Paris, avid collectors obtained posters of Chéret and other artists by bribing the billstickers or else removing the posters from the walls during the night with damp sponges.

By 1895 the poster fad was widespread. *The Chap-Book* was advertising back posters at 25 to 50 cents each when the magazine itself was selling for only 5 cents. American artists had already been recognized abroad. In London, *The Studio* published an article on Will Bradley in 1894 and Parisians saw posters by Bradley and Edward Penfield in S. Bing's first Salon de l'Art Nouveau exhibition in December 1895. That same year, Charles Scribner's Sons published the first American book on the poster movement, entitled *The Modern Poster*. To appeal to collectors, it was published in a limited edition of 1,000 copies with a signed and numbered poster by Will Bradley for each purchaser.

Important poster exhibitions were held at the Union League Club and Pratt Institute in New York, and shows followed in Boston, Chicago, and San Francisco, as well as other cities across the country. Dealers sprang up in the big cities. Brentano's, the New York bookseller, opened a poster department that specialized in imports from France. Other New York poster dealers were C. S. Pratt, Meyer Bros., and Gustave P. Fressel.

Will Bradley, *Harper's Bazar*, 1896.
This design was a rare example of the Art Nouveau style on a mass magazine poster.

Styles and the Major American Poster Artists

Two stylistic innovations—one derived from the decorative arts, the other from the graphic arts—prepared the way for the American poster renaissance. The Arts and Crafts aesthetic, which originated in England, opposed the machine production of the Industrial Revolution in favor of the personal workmanship of the Middle Ages. William Morris, the prime advocate of the Arts and Crafts philosophy, was a prodigious worker who applied his love of careful craftsmanship and ornate decoration to a multitude of endeavors, the design of chairs, wallpaper, and books among them. In France, Eugène Grasset combined the Arts and Crafts philosophy with his interest in the Japanese prints popular at the time. The style he evolved for his illustrations and posters employed flat color areas and heavily outlined two-dimensional figures. Aubrey Beardsley, too, preferred the decorative quality of line and ignored conventional modeling in favor of the juxtaposition of positive and negative masses. The term "decorative style" could be loosely applied to the work of these artists. With its roots in romanticism and its overtones of symbolism, it recognized the artist as free to interpret or ignore reality in any way he liked.

Bonnard, Toulouse-Lautrec, and Steinlen—to whose art the term "descriptive style" might be applied—also had little interest in academic notions of pictorial composition. Like Grasset, they admired the strong colors and flat spaces of the Japanese prints. From Chéret they discovered the potential of lithography for creating textured surfaces. Although interested in graphic experimentation, they also preferred to depict the reality of daily life. The subjects of their paintings, lithographs, and posters were likely to be their own friends and families rather than the nymphs, dwarfs, and angels preferred by the decorative artists.

The decorative and descriptive styles were the sources of two distinct schools of American poster design. Foremost among the decorative artists were Will Bradley, Louis Rhead, and, to some extent, Ethel Reed. The leading designer in the descriptive style was Edward Penfield. A third tendency, the "illustrative style," was represented by Maxfield Parrish. The work of the illustrative artists was not necessarily less imaginative than that of other designers but it did not reflect, or did so to a lesser degree, the new graphic movements which had developed in Europe the previous two decades.

Will Bradley

Will Bradley, whom *The Saturday Evening Post* called the "Dean of American Designers," was a self-taught artist whose early training was in the printing profession. He was born in Boston in 1868, the son of a cartoonist for a Lynn, Massachusetts, newspaper, *The Daily Item*. At the age of 12, he obtained his first job as a printer's devil with *The Iron Agitator* in Ishpeming, Michigan, where he had moved with his mother after his father's death. There he quickly learned to set type, deal with advertising

Will Bradley.

display, and make up the paper. Bradley set out for Chicago when he was 16 and found a position with Rand McNally as an apprentice in the design department. But he was dissatisfied with the job and returned to Michigan. The next year Bradley went back to Chicago and became a full-fledged designer with Knight & Leonard, the city's leading printer.

After two years with Knight & Leonard, Bradley, whose expanding talents could hardly be contained by a single firm, became a freelance designer. In 1893, the year of the World's Columbian Exposition, he received a commission from the publisher W. I. Way & Co. to design a cover and decorations for poet Harriet Monroe's paean to the Exposition, *The Columbian Ode.* Bradley's first important commission came in 1894 when *The Inland Printer,* a Chicago journal of the printing trade, asked Bradley to design a permanent cover. He did so but then persuaded the publisher to change the cover each month. This resulted in a commission for 18 *Inland Printer* covers between 1894 and 1896.

These covers, some of which were used on posters to advertise the magazine, reflect Bradley's interest in the heavily ornamented Arts and Crafts books of William Morris and the sinuous drawings of Aubrey Beardsley which were just reaching America via *The Yellow Book.* Though Bradley was called the "American Beardsley" by many critics, the appellation is unjust. There is no doubt that Bradley was influenced by the swirling lines and juxtaposed black and white masses of the English artist, but he used Beardsley's discoveries for his own purposes and within a few years had ceased to work in the Art Nouveau style.

Bradley's first poster design was probably "The Twins," which he created for Stone & Kimball's literary magazine *The Chap-Book* in the summer or fall of 1894. It was considered the first Art Nouveau poster in America and added to the wave of interest in poster collecting started by Edward Penfield's *Harper's* placards. But Bradley's decorative style was not as easy to accept as Penfield's more straightforward portrayals of the *haute bourgeoisie.* A critic writing in *The American Printer* said of "The Twins" that ". . . the funniest thing out is the 'Chap-Book' poster. No mortal man can possibly tell without deliberately investigating, what it means or what it represents. Ten feet away one would be willing to make an oath that it was a very, very red turkey gobbler very poorly represented. On closer inspection it seems to have been intended for two human beings, one at least being in a red gown very short at both ends."

Bradley's Art Nouveau poster "The Twins" *(top)* and a parody of it by Will Denslow for a *fin-de-siècle* calendar *(immediately above).*

During 1894 and 1895 Bradley did seven posters for *The Chap-Book,* all of which were extremely popular. His first book assignment also came from Stone & Kimball in late 1894: a commission for a cover, title page, page decorations, and a poster for a book of verse by Tom Hall, *When Hearts Are Trumps.* The poster was another example of the strong influence the Art Nouveau style had on Bradley at the time.

Because of his early training as a printer, Bradley's posters are distinguished by their good taste in typography which is an integral part of the design. The typography of most 1890s posters left much to be desired. Bradley's placards were notable exceptions. Bradley admired the dense ornamentation of William Morris' book pages but did not share the Englishman's love for the heavy Gothic type face that was almost impossible to read. Though he occasionally used variations of the Gothic, Bradley preferred simpler types such as the early English face, Caslon. Sometimes he designed his own lettering. The American Type Founders purchased the rights to his letters for the *Inland Printer* cover of December 1894 and cast them as a type they christened "Bradley."

Bradley's *Inland Printer* cover for December, 1894, showing the type face called "Bradley."

The WAYSIDE
Studio
at Springfield, Mass.

Mr. WILL BRADLEY begs to announce that all *Commercial Designs* bearing the above device are made at the WAYSIDE STUDIO by draughtsmen who work under his supervision.

An advertisement for The Wayside Studio, which Bradley established, along with The Wayside Press, in Springfield, Massachusetts.

Late in 1894 Bradley left Chicago for Springfield, Massachusetts, where he continued to work as a freelance designer, accepting further commissions from Chicago. He also began to do more commercial work for manufacturers of bicycles, paper, and patent medicine. After a year of freelancing, he established The Wayside Press. As its device he chose the dandelion leaf "because the dandelion is a wayside growth." Bradley had always intended to be an artist and considered printing only a wayside to achieving that end.

For a year he published his own literary and art journal, *Bradley: His Book*, one of the most elegant "little magazines" of the 1890s. Bradley was the publisher, editor, designer, illustrator, and sometimes the writer. But he was no businessman. In 1898 The Wayside Press was merged with the University Press of Cambridge, Massachusetts, and Bradley opened a design and art service in New York.

While in Massachusetts he had been an informal spokesman for the Arts and Crafts philosophy, which he applied in his heavily decorated and ornamented poster and book designs of that period. After moving to New York he simplified his style, which became better suited to the needs of mass publishing and commerce. Many years later Bradley had some second thoughts about the decorative phase of his career. In a brief autobiography written when he was in his 80s, Bradley referred to the 1890s as "a period of over-ornamentation and bad taste." Nevertheless he thought those years were ones of "leisurely contacts, kindly advice, and an appreciative pat on the back by an employer, and certainly a friendly bohemianism seldom known in the rush and drive of today."

After the turn of the century, Bradley was active as a designer, art director, writer, and even film-maker. He died in 1962 at the ripe old age of 94.

Edward Penfield

Edward Penfield, a young art director for Harper & Bros., exemplified the descriptive style in American poster design. Although Penfield had studied fine arts at the Art Students League in New York and was influenced by Toulouse-Lautrec and Steinlen, he clearly understood the aesthetic limitations of the poster form. His own simple designs, which rarely incorporated more than one or two figures, testified to his belief that "A design that needs study is not a poster, no matter how well it is executed."

For six years, with only one or two exceptions, Penfield drew the monthly placards for *Harper's*. During this period he evolved from rather lackluster designs drawn with a pen to bolder graphic statements, often created with brushstrokes and stippling on the zinc printing plates. Will Bradley admired Penfield's textural effects and emulated his techniques in some of his own posters. He paid tribute to Penfield with the statement that "in methods of reproduction, that difficult point to which so few give even a passing thought, he is a past master."

Throughout his career at *Harper's,* Penfield rarely departed from his portrayals of the rather bored and aloof members of the genteel class. Perhaps this was a stipulation of his publishers, who may have wanted posters to reflect the self-image of the monied readers they sought to attract. Penfield's placards appeared during the depression of the mid-90s, when few but the wealthy could afford the magazine's price of 35 cents. His concentration on a single social milieu and his static figures without

1894

1894

1895

1895

Harper's posters which exemplify Penfield's whimsical humor.

Edward Penfield. A self-portrait.

Maxfield Parrish.

animation or emotion led one French writer to refer to his work as "a good bourgeois cuisine which offers a profusion of substantial dishes."

Initially Penfield portrayed on every *Harper's* poster someone reading or carrying a copy of the magazine. Sometimes he handled this in a tongue-in-cheek manner, as with the October 1895 placard which shows a hunter engrossed in a copy of *Harper's* while two smiling hares perch right under his nose. The practice of displaying a copy of the magazine on each poster was picked up by other publications, including *Lippincott's*, *Scribner's*, and *St. Nicholas*.

Penfield worked almost exclusively for Harper & Bros. throughout the 1890s, doing both magazine and book posters. After 1900 he was active as a book and magazine illustrator for various companies.

Maxfield Parrish

Although Maxfield Parrish was a regular winner of poster competitions in the 1890s, his best-known designs have the quality of enlarged illustrations. They are much more detailed than the posters of Bradley or Penfield and their subtle color relationships and complexities of line and modeling, which recall early German and Flemish etchings, require careful study.

Parrish was the son of the painter and etcher Stephen Parrish. Born in Philadelphia in 1870, he studied at the Pennsylvania Academy of Fine Arts and briefly with Howard Pyle, the noted illustrator. Pyle's love of faraway lands and earlier historical periods seems to have influenced Parrish, whose own illustrations were usually located in an imaginary time and place. It must have been the romantic and escapist elements of his prints that made them so popular in households across the country after the turn of the century.

By the mid-90s Parrish had begun to achieve success as a magazine cover artist. Most of the Harper & Bros. publications as well as *Scribner's*, *St. Nicholas,* and others used his designs. His first book illustrations were done in 1897 for *Mother Goose in Prose*, the first book written by L. Frank Baum, author of *The Wizard of Oz*. Shortly thereafter he drew the covers for two novels, *Bolanyo* and *Free to Serve*. Both drawings were later used as posters, a testament to Parrish's dictum that "A book cover should certainly have a poster quality." Conversely, a drawing very similar to his prizewinning Columbia bicycle poster of 1896 was equally appropriate as a cover for *Harper's Weekly*.

Although technically accomplished, Parrish was a conservative draftsman whose posters recall the past, both in theme and style. Nevertheless, they must have been popular because anyone strolling around New York in 1896 could see "high up on the hoardings another prizewinner in the shape of a hearty and jolly little boy who has found contentment in a big bowl of oatmeal."

Maxfield Parrish, Pennsylvania Academy of the Fine Arts Poster Show, 1896.

J. C. Leyendecker, *The Interior,* 1894. An early design which shows fascination with the Art Nouveau line. This was a passing interest; his later designs were less stylized and relied on modeling in depth.

Edward Penfield, *Harper's*, 1895. This poster exemplified Penfield's use of fluid brush line. The design is enigmatic: the magazine appears to be floating on a body of water and it is difficult to imagine what the rope, which the women clutches, is connected to.

Will Bradley, *The Chap-Book*, 1895. The large letters spelling the month, "May," are barely distinguishable among the flowers.

E. B. Bird, Copeland & Day, 1896.

CINDER-PATH TALES
WILLIAM LINDSEY
John Sloan
BOSTON: COPELAND AND
DAY PRICE $1.00

John Sloan, Copeland & Day, 1896.

Frank Hazenplug, The Emerson & Fisher Co., 1896.

About the Artists

E. B. Bird.

Elisha Brown Bird (1867–1943) studied architecture at M.I.T. He did illustrations and posters for *The Inland Printer, The Chap-Book, The Red Letter, The Black Cat*, Copeland & Day, and other magazines and book publishers. He was promotion designer and cartoonist for several newspapers including *The Boston Herald* and *The New York Times*.

Caricature by Will True.

Will Bradley (1868–1962) was a self-taught artist who began as a printer's apprentice and worked in printing shops for some time before starting his career as an illustrator in Chicago. After a series of magazine covers for *The Inland Printer*, Bradley received important book and magazine poster commissions from Stone & Kimball. In 1895 he established The Wayside Press in Springfield, Massachusetts and published his own magazine, *Bradley: His Book*. Numerous requests for posters and brochures came from various manufacturers. Bradley was also a typographer and book designer. After 1900 he was active as an art director for numerous magazines including *Good Housekeeping, Collier's,* and *Metropolitan;* he wrote and illustrated a novel which was serialized in *Collier's*. He was also involved in the production of films for William Randolph Hearst.

Will Carqueville (1871-1946) was trained as a lithographer in his father's firm, Shober & Carqueville. He drew a series of posters for *Lippincott's* and *International* before going to Paris to study art. Upon his return, he established a lithography workshop in Chicago and did work for the *Chicago Tribune*, among other clients.

Charles H. Cox created a series of posters for *Bearings*, a journal for cyclists.

Arthur Wesley Dow (1857–1922) studied art in Paris and Boston, where he was introduced to Japanese art by Ernest Fenellosa at the Boston Museum of Fine Arts. He taught at Pratt Institute, the Art Students League, and Columbia Teachers College. While director of the Ipswich, Massachusetts Summer Art School he did several series of woodcuts—"Ipswich Prints" (1895) and "Along Ipswich River" (1902).

Henry B. Eddy (1872–1935) created posters for *Clips, The Criterion, The Impressonist, The New York Journal,* and *New York Ledger*, as well as for the theater.

Charles Allen Gilbert (1873–1929) studied at the Art Students League and in Paris. He illustrated books and contributed drawings to *Life* and other magazines.

Alice Russell Glenny (1858–death unknown) was a painter and sculptor who studied in New York and Paris. She designed posters for *The Buffalo Courier* and The Buffalo Academy and Fine Arts Society.

Bertram Grosvenor Goodhue (1869–1924) worked extensively as an architect but was also a noted book designer and decorator in the 1890s. He was a co-founder of *Knight Errant*, a magazine dedicated to aesthetic philosophy.

J. J. Gould was a Philadelphia artist who designed a series of posters for *Lippincott's* after Will Carqueville left the magazine. He later did some cover illustrations for *The Saturday Evening Post*.

Eugène Grasset (1841–1917) was a French decorative artist who painted, did book illustrations, and designed tapestries, stained glass, posters, and mosaics. Grasset's first American poster was for *Harper's* magazine.

Theo Hampe. Biographical information unavailable.

Self-portrait.

Ernest Haskell (1876–1925) designed posters for *Truth, The New York World, The Critic, The New York Journal,* and for books. In 1897–98 he studied in Paris and exhibited at the Salon of the Société Nationale. Though he was known for his landscapes and watercolors, he continued to do magazine illustrations, particularly for *Harper's*. After the turn of the century, he gained a reputation for his etchings.

Frank Hazenplug (1873–death unknown) was staff artist for Stone & Kimball. He designed *Chap-Book* posters and several book and exhibition placards.

Joseph Christian Leyendecker (1874–1971) was an illustrator and advertising artist who came to America from Germany as a young boy. After studying at the Chicago Art Institute and learning engraving with a commercial firm, he spent several years studying art in Paris. Leyendecker won the *Century* poster competition in 1896 and contributed posters and magazine covers to *Scribner's, The Inland Printer, Interior Design,* and *The Saturday Evening Post*. His best-known advertisements were for *Chap-Book*. After 1900 he worked extensively for *Collier's* and Arrow collars and Chesterfield cigarettes.

Will Low (1853-1932) was a figure and genre painter who studied in Paris with Gérôme and Carolus Duran. He was also active as a book illustrator and designed posters for *Scribner's*, The National Academy of Design, and The Society of American Artists.

 **Florence Lundborg** (1871-1949) is best known for her colorful woodcut posters advertising *The Lark* of San Francisco. Primarily a painter, she studied in San Francisco, Italy, and France. An important commission was the group of wall paintings she did for the California Building at the Panama-Pacific Exhibition.

Blanche McManus (1870-death unknown), after a sojourn in Paris, returned to America in 1893 and set up a studio in Chicago. She did book and magazine illustrations as well as posters for several book publishers. After the turn of the century, she moved to Paris where she continued to draw for books and magazines.

Frank Arthur Nankivell (1865-1959), an Australian, spent several years in Asia before reaching San Francisco in 1894. His drawings appeared in the San Francisco paper *The Call*, and in *The Echo*, founded by his friend Percival Pollard in Chicago. Nankivell moved to New York in 1896 and contributed illustrations to *The New York Journal* and *Puck*. Posters were designed for the *Journal*, *The Clack Book*, *The Echo*, and several book publishers. The artist later studied portrait painting and worked for the *Ladies' Home Journal*.

Sketch by L.M.Glackens.

Richard Felton Outcault (1863-1928) was the creator of "The Yellow Kid," the first comic panel to appear regularly in an American newspaper, *The New York Journal*. His "Yellow Kid" posters were known all over New York. Another famous Outcault comic series was "Buster Brown."

Maxfield Parrish (1870-1966) studied at the Pennsylvania Academy of Fine Arts and briefly with Howard Pyle. He was awarded prizes in several major poster competitions in the 1890s. Commissions for magazine covers and posters came from *Harper's Bazar*, *Harper's Weekly*, *Harper's Roundtable*, *Scribner's*, *St. Nicholas*, and others. Book posters were done for Way & Williams and Copeland & Day. Parrish did extensive commercial work, including advertisement for Fiske Tires and Edison Mazda. After 1900 he created many covers for *Collier's*, *Life*, and *Ladies' Home Journal*.

Examples of early (left) and late (right) signatures.

Caricature by Hy Mayer.

Edward Penfield (1866-1925) studied at the Art Students League before serving as Art Director for various Harper periodicals from 1881 to 1901. He designed monthly posters for *Harper's* from 1893 to 1898 and also did some book posters for Harper & Bros. during this period. After 1900 he continued as a book and magazine illustrator. Two books of his drawings were published: *Holland Sketches* (1907) and *Spanish Sketches* (1911).

Edward Henry Potthast (1857-1927) studied painting in America and Europe. He designed a famous poster for the Barnum & Bailey circus featuring a bareback rider. Another of his placards won honorable mention in *The Century's* poster contest in 1896. As an artist, he was recognized for his seascapes.

Ethel Reed (1876-death unknown) studied art in the Boston area and was already established as an illustrator by the age of 18. Though she did occasional newspaper and magazine placards, she was best known for the book posters designed for the Boston literary publishers Copeland & Day and Lamson, Wolffe & Co. Several of the books for which she did posters featured her own illustrations. The artist was not heard from after 1898.

 Louis John Rhead (1857-1926) was born in England and educated at the South Kensington Art School and in Paris. In 1883 he came to New York to work for the D. Appleton Co. as an illustrator. He received early poster commissions in 1889 and 1890 from *The Century*, *Harper's*, and *St. Nicholas*. From 1891 to 1894 he studied in London and Paris where he was strongly influenced by the work of Eugène Grasset. The Wunderlich Gallery in New York gave Rhead a one-man exhibition in 1895 and another show followed in 1897 in Paris at the Salon des Cent. Rhead created numerous posters for the *New York Sun* and the *Journal*. Magazine and book posters were designed for *Scribner's*, Copeland & Day, and L. Prang & Co.; additional posters were done for various manufacturers. After 1900, Rhead was mainly active as a book illustrator and wrote several books on fishing.

J. A. Schweinfurth. Biographical information unavailable.

 **John Sloan** (1871-1952) studied at the Pennsylvania Academy of Fine Arts and worked as an illustrator for *The Philadelphia Inquirer* before he was able to pursue a career as a painter and printmaker. He belonged to the group of New York painters, "The Eight." As an illustrator, he had drawings published in *Everybody's Magazine*, *Harper's Weekly*, *Collier's*, and *The Chap-Book*. Posters were designed for *Moods*, *The Echo*, and Copeland & Day.

John Twachtman (1853-1902), one of the first American Impressionists, studied painting in Cincinnati and Europe and was known for his landscapes.

J. J. Gould, *Lippincott's*, 1897.

Epilog

The innovation and experimentation that characterized the best posters of the 1890s was due in large part to the fact that many of the designers were young men and women with no commitment to the academic traditions that preceded them. The most dedicated of the young poster artists were interested in developing their own styles and had the good fortune to begin their careers at a time when so many opportunities existed for trying out new ideas and techniques. Most of the artists were still in their twenties when the poster movement reached its peak. J. C. Leyendecker was 22 when he won the *Century* poster contest in 1896 and Ethel Reed was only 19 when booksellers first began to display her placards.

By the end of the decade the interest in poster collecting had waned. The literary book and magazine publishers who had been responsible for so many elegant posters were out of business and the commercial publishers tended to favor a more realistic style. Though artists produced noteworthy posters after the turn of the century, there was no longer the sense of an artistic movement that one felt in the 1890s. Edward Penfield, Will Bradley, and Louis Rhead continued as commercial illustrators but designed few posters. Maxfield Parrish's dreamy paintings hung in homes throughout America and J. C. Leyendecker became a popular advertising illustrator and magazine cover artist. Some of the poster designers of the 1890s, particularly Ethel Reed, Frank Hazenplug, and J. J. Gould, were no longer heard from.

The American poster renaissance was brief but its effect on the visual arts was permanent. The poster in the 1890s was the chief medium through which Americans were introduced to the new European graphic styles, particularly Art Nouveau and the post-impressionist lithographic experiments. The enthusiasm for the artistic poster may also be seen as an early phase of the loosening of academic ties that culminated in the total freedom of the 1913 Armory Show.

The Modern Poster was published in 1895 in a limited edition, with signed and numbered posters by Will Bradley.

The Chap-Book

1   (*preceding page*) Will Bradley, *The Chap-Book*, "The Twins," 1894.

2   Will Bradley, Stone & Kimball, 1894.

WHEN HEARTS
ARE TRUMPS ♥
BY TOM HALL

3   Louis Rhead, *Century Magazine*, 1894.

4   John Twachtman, Stone & Kimball, 1894.

THE DAMNATION of THERON WARE
or ILLUMINATION
BY HAROLD FREDERIC·
PUBLISHED BY STONE & KIMBALL.

5   Will Bradley, Overman Wheel Co., 1895.

6 Will Bradley, *The Chap-Book*, "Pegasus," 1895.

7   Will Bradley, Whiting Paper Co., 1895.

8   Will Bradley, *The Chap-Book*, 1895.

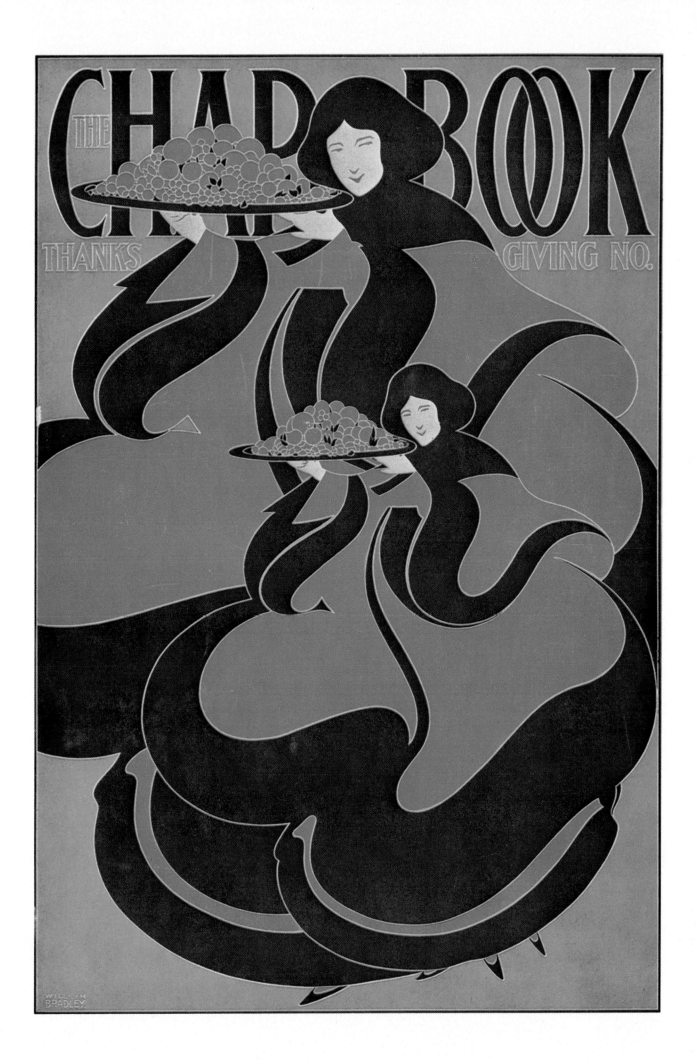

9   Will Carqueville, *Lippincott's,* 1895.

10   Arthur Dow, *Modern Art,* 1895.

modernArt

EDITED BY J. M. BOWLES
PUBLISHED BY L. PRANG & CO.

Arthur W Dow

WOMENS

EDITION

(BUFFALO)

COURIER.

SCRIBNER'S

FICTION NUMBER

The Adventures of Captain Horn

by Frank R. Stockton

Charles Scribner's Sons Publishers

J.E. Rhodes, New York.

15   Blanche McManus, Lamson, Wolffe & Co., 1895.

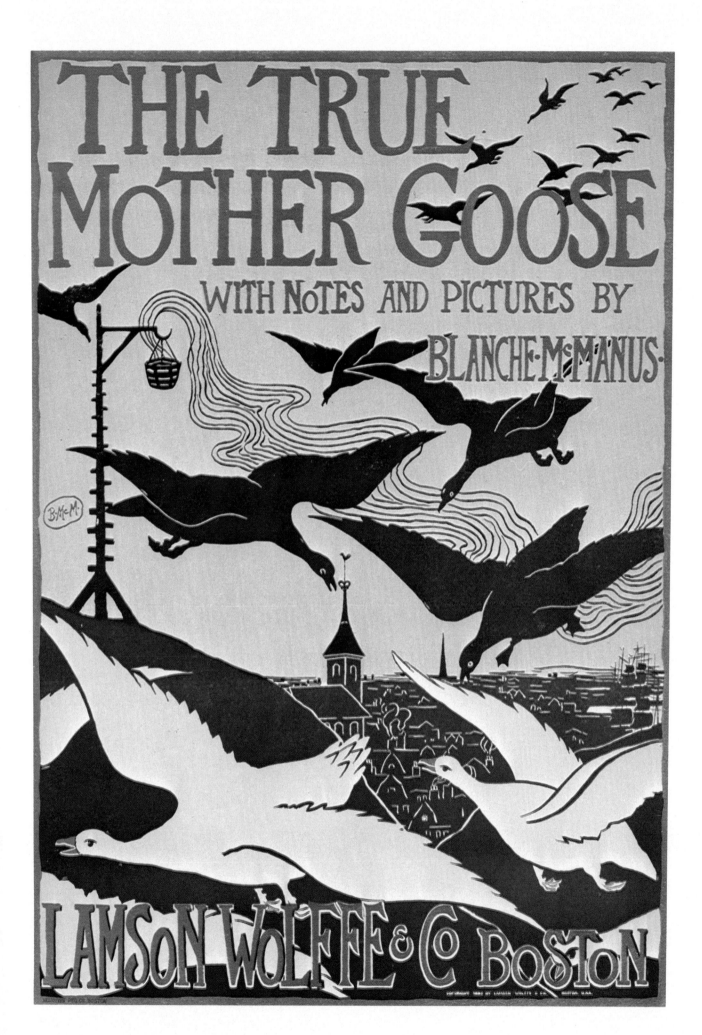

16   R. F. Outcault, *The New York World* (?), c. 1895.

17   Edward Penfield, Waltham Mfg. Co., c. 1895.

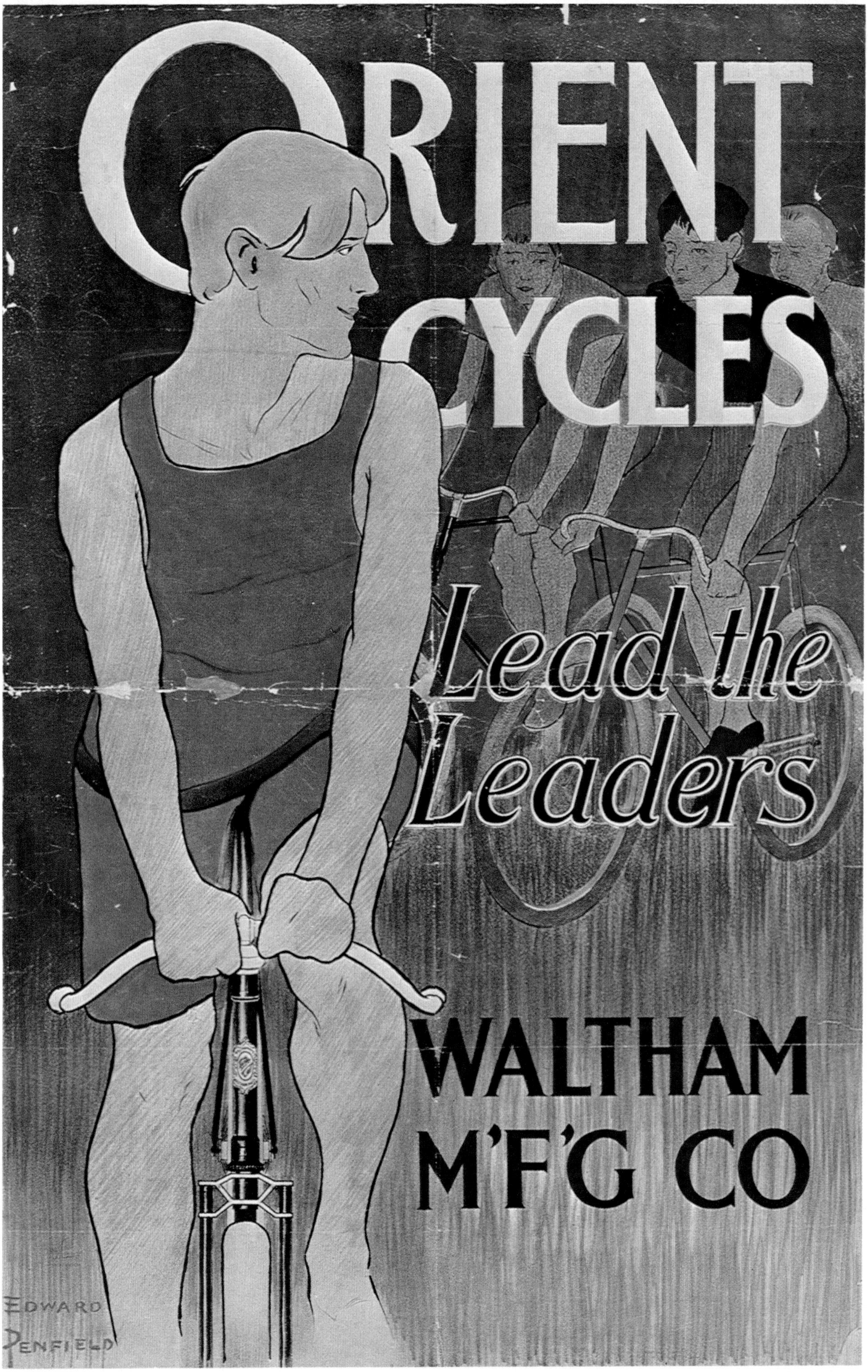
ORIENT
CYCLES
Lead the Leaders
WALTHAM
M'F'G CO
EDWARD PENFIELD

18   Ethel Reed, Copeland & Day, 1895.

ARABELLA AND ARAMINTA STORIES BY GERTRVDE SMITH WITH XV PICTVRES BY ETHEL REED

BOSTON COPELAND AND DAY
PRICE $2.00 NET

19 Louis Rhead, *The New York Sun*, 1895.

20   Louis Rhead, Mandeville and King, c. 1895.

MANDEVILLE AND KING

SUPERIOR
FLOWER·SEEDS
·ROCHESTER·N·Y·

21   Louis Rhead, *The New York Sun*, c. 1895.

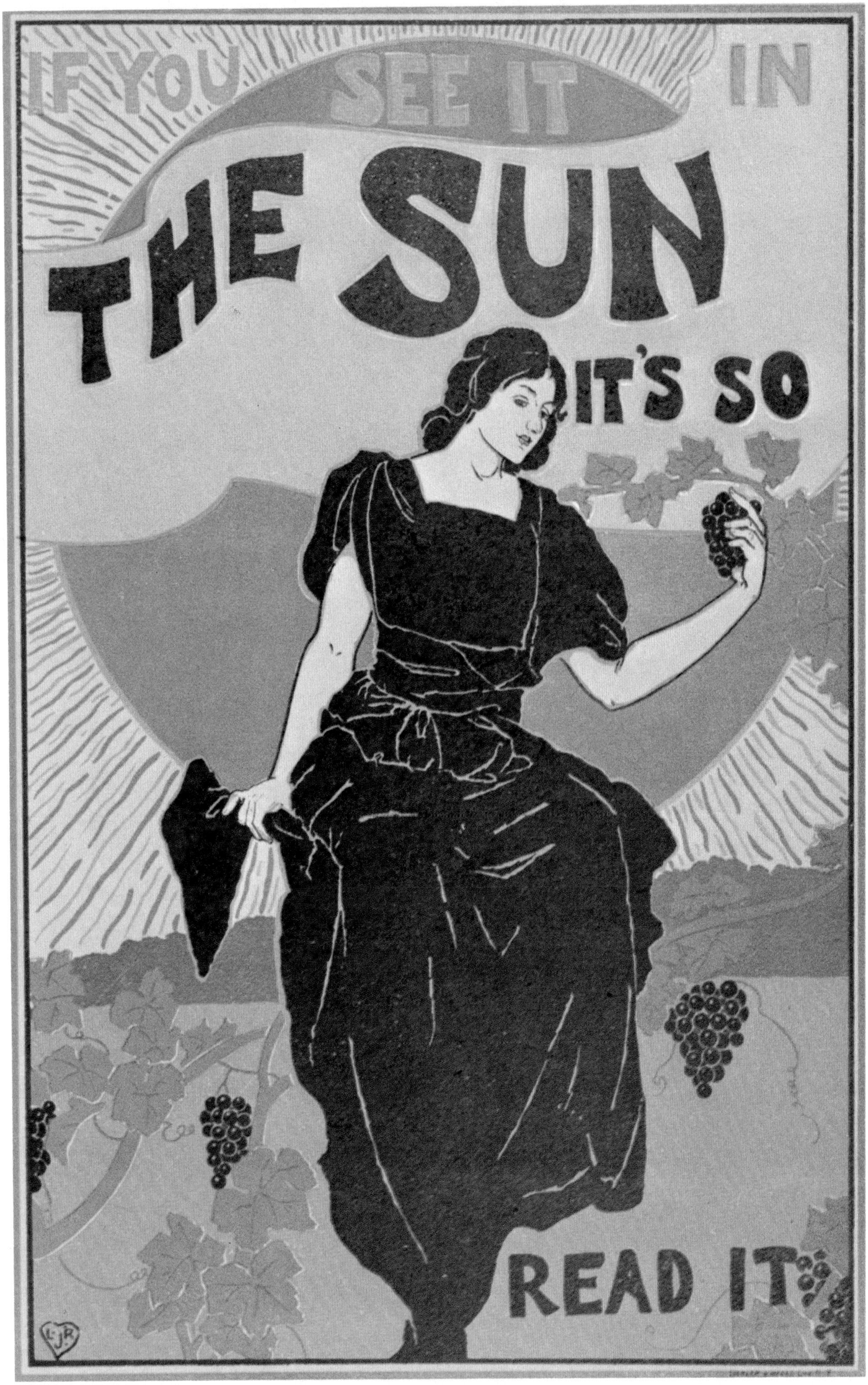
IF YOU SEE IT IN
THE SUN
IT'S SO
READ IT

FOR SALE HERE.

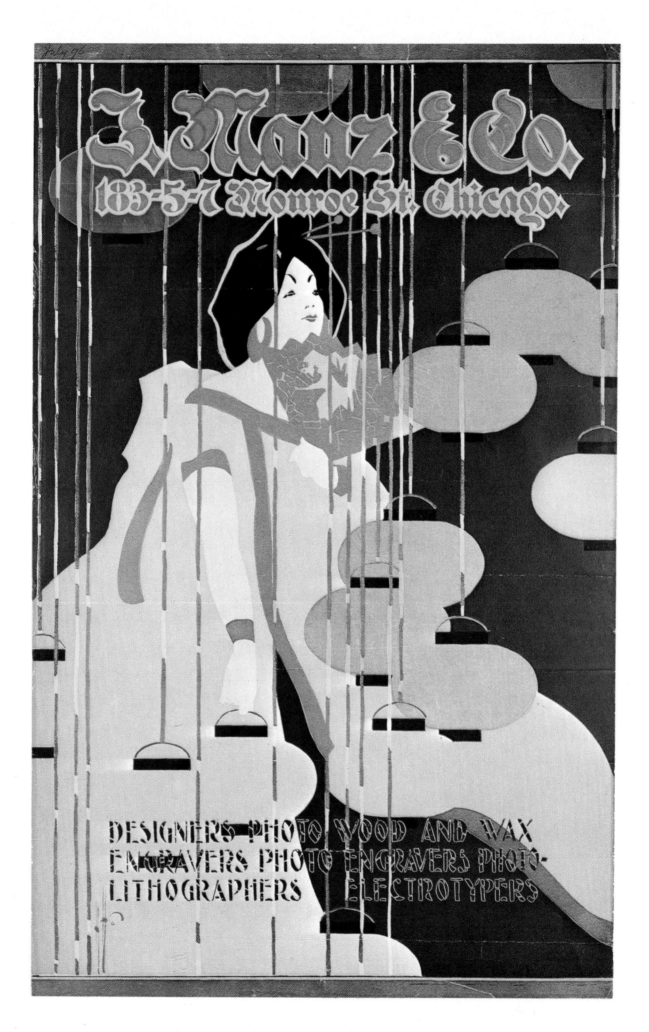

25   Will Bradley, *Bradley: His Book*, Wayside Press, 1896.

26 Charles Cox, *Bearings,* c. 1896.

27   Arthur Dow, Japanese print exhibition, 1896.

28   Bertram Grosvenor Goodhue, portrait exhibition, 1896.

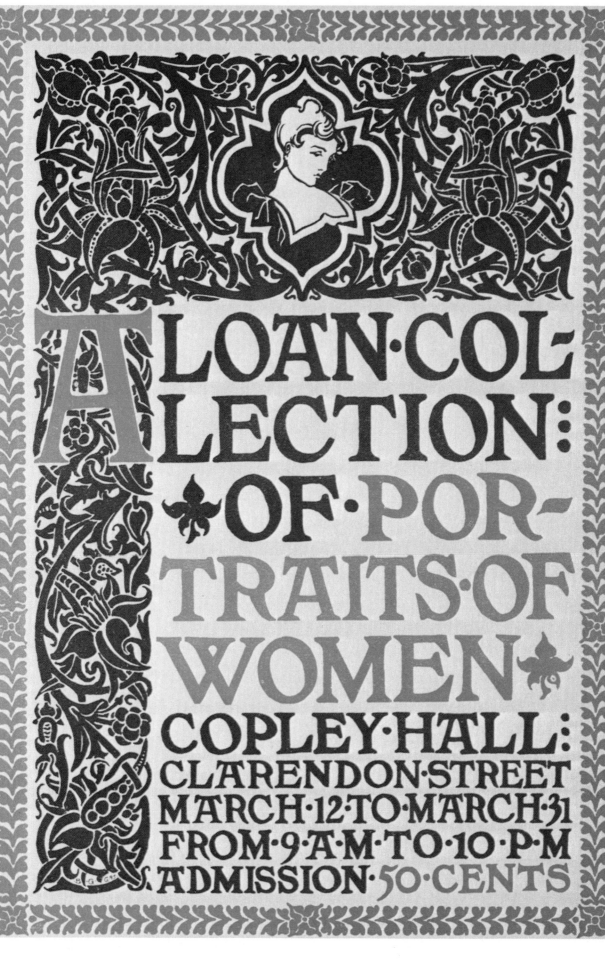

A LOAN·COL-
LECTION:
·OF·POR-
TRAITS·OF
WOMEN·
COPLEY·HALL:
CLARENDON·STREET
MARCH·12·TO·MARCH·31
FROM·9·A·M·TO·10·P·M
ADMISSION·50·CENTS

29   Theo Hampe, *St. Nicholas*, 1896.

August

St. NICHOLAS

30   Ernest Haskell, *Truth,* 1896.

31 Frank Hazenplug, *The Chap-Book*, "The Green Lady," 1896.

32   J. C. Leyendecker, *The Century*, 1896.

33 Florence Lundborg, *The Lark*, 1896.

THE CENTURY

Midsummer Holiday Number. August.

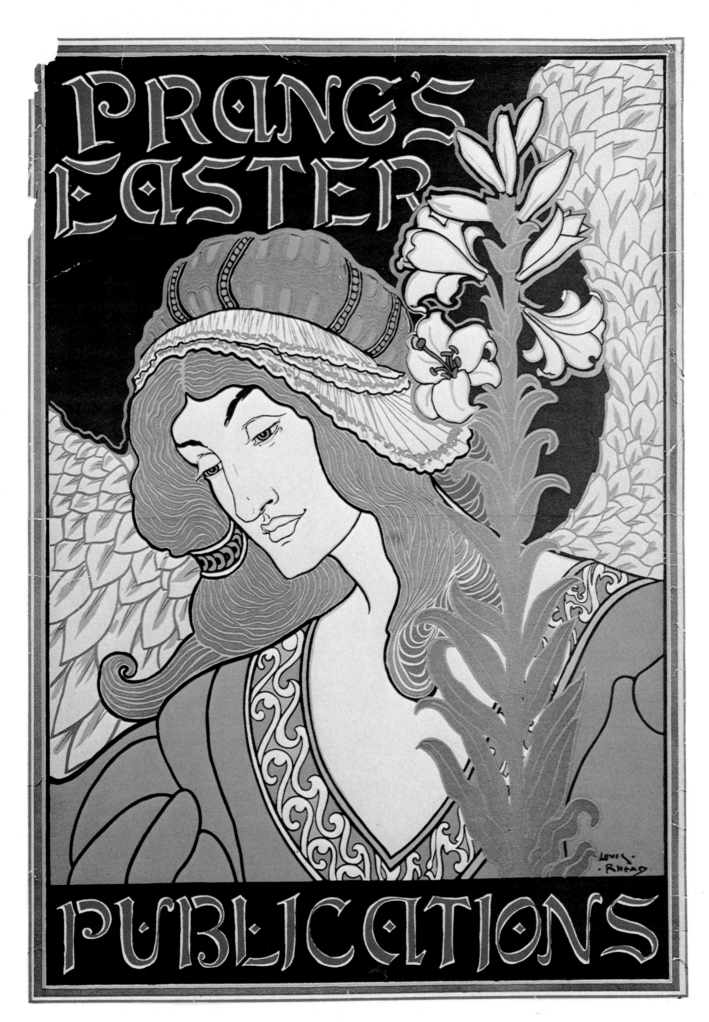

37   Louis Rhead, *The Century*, 1896.

38   Alice Glenny, Buffalo Fine Arts Academy and Society of Artists Exhibition, 1897.

40   Frank Nankivell, *The New York Journal,* 1897.

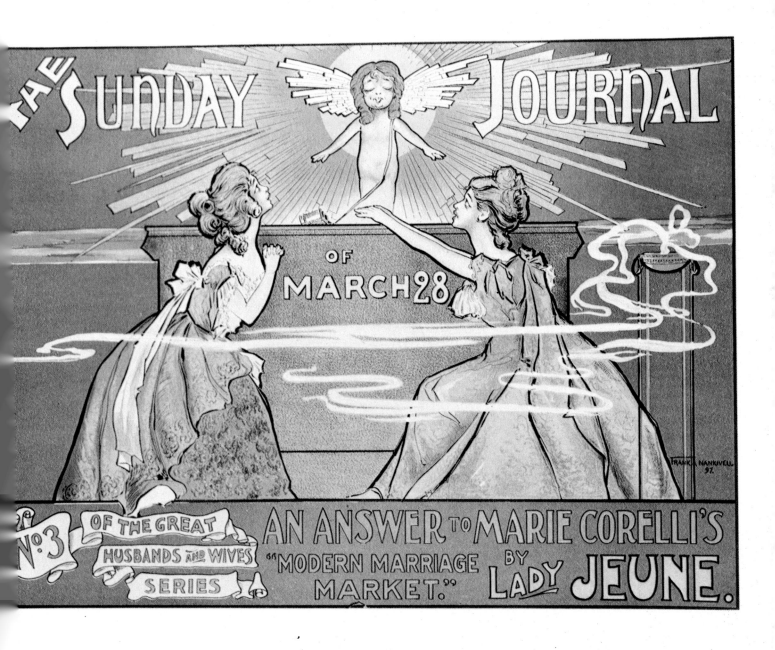

41   Maxfield Parrish, The Adlake Camera, 1897.

THE ADLAKE CAMERA

4" x 5", with **twelve** plate holders , **$12.**

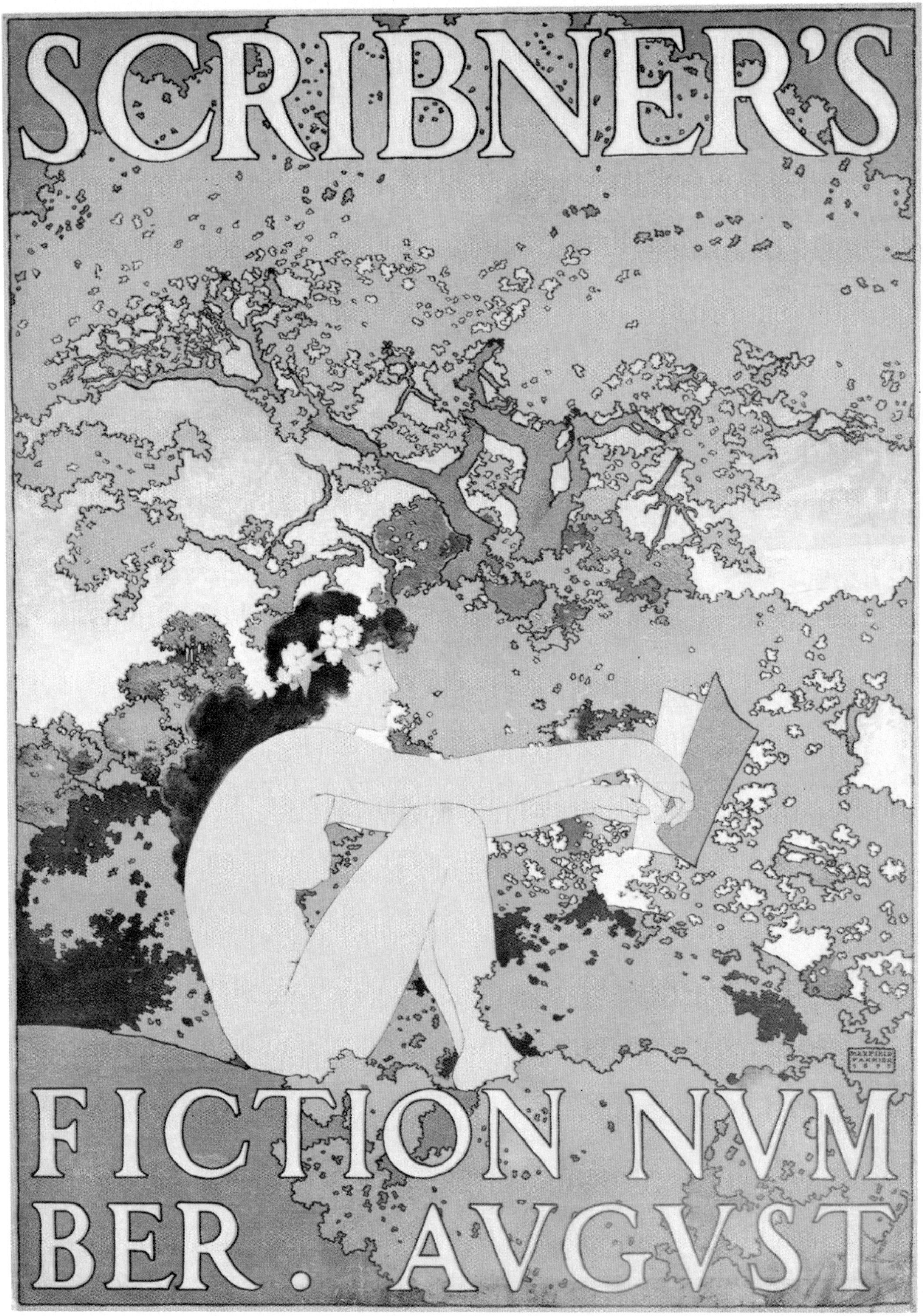
SCRIBNER'S
MAXFIELD
PARRISH
1897
FICTION NVM
BER. AVGVST

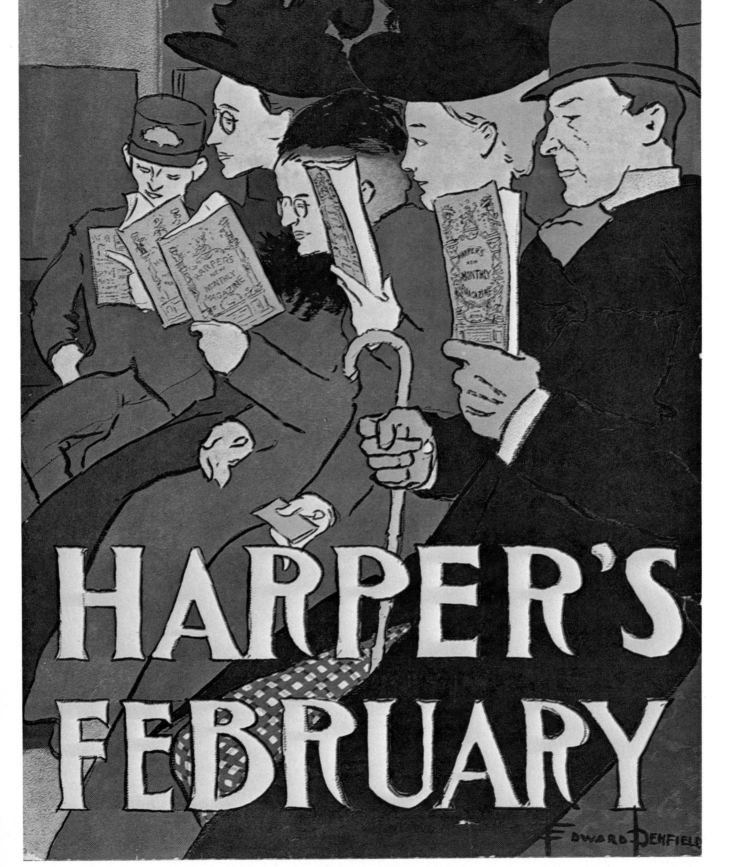

45   Edward Penfield, Harper & Bros., 1897.

47   J. A. Schweinfurth, Little, Brown & Co., 1897.

QVO·VADIS·

A·NARRATIVE·OF·THE TIME·OF·NERO·BY· HENRY·K·SIENKIEWICZ·

·PVBLISHED·BY·LITTLE· BROWN·&·Cº·BOSTON·

48   C. Allan Gilbert, *Scribner's*, 1898.

WELLESLEY COLLEGE
BY MISS GOODLOE
ILLUSTRATED IN THE
MAY SCRIBNER'S

Index to Full-Page Reproductions